THE ARDORS

Kathleen Peirce

AUSABLE PRESS
2004

Cover art: "Asylum" by Julie Speed
Gouache and collage, 2002
Collection of Carrie Bills

Design and composition by Ausable Press
The type is Adobe's Garamond 3 with Trajan Titling.
Cover design by Rebecca Soderholm

Published by
AUSABLE PRESS
1026 HURRICANE ROAD
KEENE NY 12942
www.ausablepress.org

Library of Congress Cataloging-in-Publication Data
Peirce, Kathleen 1956—
The ardors / by Kathleen Peirce.–1st ed.
p. cm.
ISBN 1-931337-19-5 (hardcover : alk. paper)
ISBN 1-931337-20-9 (pbk. : alk. paper)
I. Title.
PS3566.E34A73 2004
811'.54–DC22
2004000014

for Joseph

THE ARDORS

CONTENTS

FONDLE PEARLS AND THEY'RE QUICK TO FLY

Outermost nacreous layer where reflection was
made constantly to bend is how the pearl turned,
even when at rest, like the simple hunger of the dead
brought to bear on the smell of baking bread,
then felt by us as peacefulness
when bending toward a loaf, a slice, a crumb. In this way
we felt acted on as well as left alone, at every turn
reawakening with variation,
with the sense of previous bearings
as well as those we lacked. We saw ourselves
not in the pearls we found, but in the pearls too deep,
too underneath, that went unseen
and were increased. These lay together in our minds;
with these we made adornments for someone.

DREAMING OF SLEEP

It was a human place. On either side
young women and young men held manmade things
contrived for widening their lives. Some held,
by way of opened books, a separate and singular repose
so much less tense than the precision of any open flower.
There were no flowers; every torso was arranged
to complement the object of its thought. It was understood
the dead could no more lean above guitars or books,
or turn their heads and speak, or list their heads to weep
again. It was among the lucid restive ones we moved,
accompanied by who was ours, through wide halls dense with
empty ornate wooden beds, into a room in red which held
the one bed and a window, where we looked away, blurred
as if two books at once were being read to us.

FROM INSIDE

Some weather made the windows pearled,
and our rooms occurred around us with more gentleness
than on the other days, far more than nights we woke
without meaning to. We'd seen
blunt-ended feathers from the blue-black tails of crows
land, quill down, among the angular and secretive
pinecones in a neighbor's yard,
or, sleeping on a mountainside,
we felt aware of hidden birds aware of us
as we woke and looked at something, anything;
or coming down the stairs, we heard, in olden clock-notes,
in the four strikes of a quarter hour, the promise of
a cumulative truth, each event
building more events. But when our rooms were quieted
we also heard the slight, interior, wooden, pre-chime knock
and thought the world had signaled us
from where the other worlds were hid.

FROM UNDERNEATH

When we were untouched by human voices,
we could hear music played, and we were not unlike
the selves we brought to animals
whose presences were instruments of love
almost without fail. We saw birds every day;
before we slept we often thought of how those fly
who fly at night, not the dark topfeathers
serrating another dark, but the pale
underfeathers hidden by a wing that could, and had
glanced back. Fish also kept a paleness underneath;
don't think we weren't afraid. Our stillness
was pearl-stillness; if we were radiant
it was a radiance accrued while having been contained.
We wondered why to shell is to pry out. Music was beautiful,
fathomless in a way we understood, the notes most often
falling at the end like words in sentences, pearls in water,
animals, blue sky. We understood that in the time it took
each chord to play, some of us would die. Some continued
being held; others were holding still and listening.

WITH EYES CLOSED

Nor did we ever tire of saying what the light was like,
especially when full on in the fall, in afternoon, when
warm light passed through air the ground made cold,
from where dawn could be remembered even if slept through,
dawn the diadem through which gold passed
and found, late afternoon, our turned-up faces with eyes closed;
how unlike being passed across *that* was.
At sunset, the same sun seemed all about itself, and if on us,
we felt it as a stain but going, gone. Speech about light
rose to, fell from who weakened when love
passed away. *Woman writing on water*
was the first gesture we were saddened by.
Woman writing in blood was next, and last,
to which we later added one worse thing,
but that was very late, and dark, and hard to see.

BLACK PEARL

The arm is lowered, the wrist is flexed
as to present the palm more or less
parallel to the ground – not unlike
a natural gesture of supressing. This way
we showed we loved, not the dead,
but ourselves remembering what those
once living thought about,
those now dissolved by what-nots making up the dirt,
blurred and engulfed maybe the same as any object
approached in increments by light, and we were changed
softly as when we thought about the stars
when the sky was blue. There were lilies
named star-gazer; their buds were fits of color
pushing into light, but their scent, it seemed,
was another way to think of radiance, like thoughts
we thought the dead once had, the dead
the earth and heaven had made far from us.

THE ROOMS

When we dreamed of rooms
we knew that entering can cause a place to be,
as when a pearl is a worm's dream,
accrued by a layering of substances outside itself
of which it is the cause. So it was with our
dream-rooms, which we always felt we had
discovered more than made.
In our dream-rooms, our mothers were young again,
while the fur on the magnolia pods remained the same
as in our wakeful lives, and water did, wearing water's face.
Hallways, doorways. We were helpless going in,
unable to die there, and when we woke
we knew we had been shaped, not loved
as pearls are loved; we were not removed.

ESTEEM

Nor was there time to balance the indignities
with acts of grace, or to enumerate either
in the drowse of our pre-sleep. Ours was a gluttony
we struggled to feel shame for. Either way,
another would pull up for our heaviness a
thin wire chair, or heap the dining table
with pastel strands of freshwater pearls, or
in night-water, open hands our heads floated toward.
That was readiness; that was one of the colors in the dark.

HALL OF LIGHT

In the way the orange canary's phrase protruded
in the quiet of the room, there was the passing of
a sunflower seed across a gap between two cardinals
outside, and the final color of the grass achieved
the rosiest of its browns. In the way a solitary thought
keeps hid a chamber, lit only by reflections
on its inner walls of jade and gold, we could feel
absence as a bird's indifference to the color
of a leaf, being the most lucid thing among a field of leaves,
or a hawk's indifference to the passage of a labial cloud
above its back, or a breast-cloud, or a mouth. Do you hear
how morning feels? There is singing where you are?

OF AIR

It was rare for our bodies to be met
on every surface by the air
though it was air that seemed to hold
what might hook briefly everywhere,
air where the past might have
to go, retouching us as bad wind on bad days,
calm on the good, though it was wind that showed us
time made physical, and it was wonderful to stand
so easily inside a thing. We never tried to heal ourselves
by drawing one another's body through, the way we had
in water, but thinking so revealed the birds as pearls of air
slid across our view on cords of their own understanding,
who flocked as pearls appear to roll themselves toward rest.
And then the way we thought about our dead made sense,
lowering them again into the folds, loving whatever touched,
remembering the unseen had touched us differently;
things seen had resembled other things.

TIME SHALL NOT LOSE OUR PASSAGES

And yet there were no wings. When we tried
to imagine our dead with feathers on
we felt ridiculous. But when we thought of them
as feathery, the afterlife made sense.
It was a string of rainy days that showed us
how a wall can be passed through,
where, after time, through an open window
small frogs will jump at night, and in the morning,
snails on the glass inside and out.
And so our dream lives crossed into our wakeful bodies,
and we began to touch without a goal. When we spoke,
we described a dream of flight where we rose singly
in air as though remembering. When we woke again
we saw our children at the mirror close their eyes
to try to see themselves with their eyes closed,
and we were more reminded than amazed. We saw
the afterlife in what they did, and sight was feathery.

ACCESSION

We wanted to approach each other from our bodies
the way one good day approached,
or how one thought first moved us
when we knew black as saturation,
not as absence of the colors.
We felt ourselves made strange
and asked to be approached as we approached,
not as a mirror will appear to move
toward a moving form
but like a color from the vegetal world,
or an entrance, or a girl as tall
as the knob on the door which is her door,
who feels her thought of blackberries
very near her pleasure in the berries themselves,
which are beyond her sight
in the sidegarden, and she told not to touch.

MEASURE

We were wide; the way was narrow;
we could feel trees ripening, cherries or no,
and we found the pleasures of dreamlife
unrecognizable as fruitful
except inside ourselves. Things increased
by layering: trees ripened, it got dark;
it was too difficult to wish for less,
to clear ourselves away in readiness for a future happiness
where we might be reformed as something lit and slight and clear.
Some days we felt each seed complicit with us, privately,
and gemstones were, and rain. So it was strange
when we saw tall trees make water-movements in the air,
or we saw a peony withhold one blade of fire,
a pearl's interstice with dirt, rain's tongue.
We felt what entered others cross to pass into our sleep
whether we were known or not,
to show how slight, how variable any body was.

PEARL

Sometimes we wanted to last longer
with our eyes closed, to know a day
as each of us had known interiors
of each mother once,
or to exaggerate our dream lives
into shared experience, or to see
if darkness projected on an object
altered it, as we seemed altered every night.
So we were pearls, or tried to feel ourselves
to be the thoughts of pearls. It was difficult
being still among the most still things,
but where we found bodies of trees attached
to earth, we were reassured, except their leaves
were like our dreams, unapproachable as a mass,
and each carrying the tense fragility of skin.
Then things stopped resembling us
the more we touched or thought of them.
By the time we could be carried into water,
formless, viscous, scented with the deaths,
we were most afraid, and most aware that to be held
is different than to be healed, but not by much.
Which led us to behold, and our eyes looked,
and some could see beloveds everywhere.

THE BELLS BREAK DOWN THEIR TOWER

If we hadn't been lonely, could we have sensed,
both underwater and in air, the tendencies
of flickering? So many moved that way:
fish, wing, hand, star, branch at sunrise,
branch in water, branch on fire.
We were constant, or felt that our will was,
even as we pulsed and blinked, and it was
our constancy that made us want to enter
smaller things with confidence,
and larger things with fear. So it was easier
to feel more longing for our equals than our gods.
A single snail baffled us. Had it made its shell with its secretions
or had it found itself? And then of course the snail
crept away. But the pearls we strung were lunar, luminous,
tellurian, and still. Draped across a woman's breast,
they tempered us, who were constantly drawn to sites of sustenance
without the memory of having eaten there, where gradually
we found ourselves most often trembling and wavering and loose.

WELLS

As our days emptied of chores
there was the gradual return of constancy
stillness is so often thought to bear
the beauty of. But it was not always beautiful
when the smallest acts took on
the weight of the profound. As when
two travelers in a vast environment
experience increasing lengths of time
before responding to the simplest of sentences,
what came was sometimes tedious.
But this brought on two beauties
new to us; one was the clarity of smaller things:
pinfeathers extruded on the face of a finch,
hooks on burs, the stinger visible inside
the living bee, the confusion as to whether
the snake's tip is the beginning or the end.
The other was the perfection of monotony
like water in a glass, water stretching in the rain,
water enlarged enough to swallow us.
And if we let go our pearls
one by one into our wells, it was to reenact
our disappearances into interiors that held
what we thought of as our origin, but the structures
we understood as plain, and made by us.

WATERCOLOR

If it rained, we were sometimes drawn closer
to the windows as they changed,
glass veils brought to wavering,
from where we sometimes held another water
in another glass, and put a flame-shaped brush tip in
to take water into color, color to a page.
What to paint? Most went always first to blue,
most of us, after a bath, dried off a
shoulder first. Why *off*? What happened
to the girls taught to make bobbin lace
who watched, dulled or transfixed,
the dry place threads caught in air,
never their hands that made our hands
seem like the unmet lungs of the unborn,
or like peach blossoms so long passed into fruit
they had withdrawn to the suspended heaviness
of seeds? Some days it rained inside of us,
no brush touched down, no paper drank for us,
whose teeth, each time, felt strange
at the dry furrow on a peach. Blue for water,
blue for sky, tears for rain.

JAWS

Filled to its vaulted roof with flower petals,
it did seem less an aperture for the Lord
and more something of our making,
we who were counted, who had known countless
occasions we might have otherwise been swallowed by.
Being so drawn to what lay across the surfaces,
when we approached we felt ourselves
lit by beauty as wetness is so often lit. We knew
what followed as the seed of all belief, and perfected as we were
by shared experience, what else was there to do but see the sea
of anemones and trout lilies at our feet, with
sea lavender, sea rockets, and virgin's bower everywhere
to pick, and prop the hinge of our undoing.

QUIET LINES

We wanted to be seen by our mothers
but our mothers were falling down,
and though we tried to think of falling
as the inversion of ascent, our thinking failed
for we had not ascended very far,
even by middle age, or if we had,
we had been taught to feel our heights discreetly,
as titmice might feel while waiting in a cypress
for the rain to stop, and wasn't fall
beautiful, the cypress leaves more feather-like in brown.
When our mothers entered the familiar rooms
and looked at us, and knew not who we were,
we were not anonymous, we were more shell than pearl
is all, opened to the limit at the hinge: wings for a doll to wear.
No pearl; pearls roll away. So we remember them.

SLOW SONG

For the women who loved to part
their legs for cellos, there were men
who played the flute. For the blue jay
whose head-feathers were tapped forward by a gust
there was all of air to turn around in.
But it was difficult to feel the aptitude for motion
in our monuments, and our monumental feelings
held the weight of telling us apart. We loved the motion
as largesse passed by or in, but as we aged,
the monumental was brought on more frequently
by smaller motions happening at once, as when we watched
a flake of salmon, salmon-colored, lifted to the actual mouth
of one who'd kissed us in a dream. Our wholeness seemed
composed, and we could sense the parts if not assemble them,
while words played out their fullness at our mouths
in a chorale of stops and starts. Thus we were revealed
and contained, and thus the stem was dragged across the strings.

DREAM OF FLIGHT

When joy returned to us in sleep
sometimes it took the shape of flying,
as though by having taken curves in,
in wakefulness, with our eyes or mouths,
our dreams were seeded with such arcs
as wings can make, or the arc of feeling pleasure
that was mirrored in the shape of wings
as well as what wings do. Sometimes our flights were heavy
like a waltz or the outline of a pear, and we glided in a way
corvids understand over the bodies of their food,
but sometimes we would lift high, as though
we were not being lifted, but had loved the world enough
that we could know it further any way we liked,
and it was those dreams we loved to speak about,
by whose forms we were moved differently and
were made multiple where we had thought to disappear.

DELECTATIO MOROSA

Again among burned grasses, one gentian-colored floral spray.
So we kept returning to scenes where highness and lowness
might be exchanged or blent, scenes of triumphal gratitude,
the thanker equally humble and profound, and the thanked
like a dog eyeing a man with recognition while feeling
that to have a tail is wonderful. Much of what we saw
restored us this way, although some we took
to be female cardinals were pyrrhuloxia,
and we named the addition of a pigment to a shade
a subtractive mix, and some began again to think of angels
as our help. We tried to keep ourselves
from the bodily immersions where graves abound,
as we would have been as flames suspended in a glass of water,
or water hung inside a pearl of dirt. It was enough
that so much tore the air and left the air unchanged. It was
too much. And the worst is, there was difference all the time.

LINEN NAPKIN

Woven for cutting, cut for sewing,
sewn to wear away, yes,
but first worn upon
and again upon, passed across
so many mouths like a middle name spoken
as the first name of other women,
or many times across one mouth
as a middle name quietly worn;
then, years later, sewn into again, with
floss following like a body pulled by love or
someone else's death in moments
sudden and exact and following the memory
of what a lily looked like, or a rose.

FROM THE MIDDLE

We were asleep when a voice made the water-weeds turn and
wave away from our shoulders, our eyes; then there was
only empty water, and finally the common air
of wakefulness where we saw women embroider
while looking up at us, each of them pale with age.
We exhaled onto every sour thread,
not out of love for the sewn lily, the sewn rose,
but in the manner of winter passing from the mouth
while the mouth is watched, a mouth more steady than
false smoke. Even so, we had nothing to say;
we believed the moment was sweet but wouldn't hold,
that we would not be gripped
by an awareness of the ground, belief in heaven,
recollection of a scent. Their hands ascended toward
the ceiling, turned, descended toward the floor.
There was the slightest song. They offered to weep
for us; they exhaled the scent of funeral carnations.

THE MYSTERIES

. . . noble mystery differs from ignoble, in being a veil thrown between us and something definite, known, and substantial; but the ignoble mystery is a veil cast before chaos, the studious concealment of Nothing.

—Ruskin

Then two watched as one drew place exactly from its body
from what had long been named a spinneret, where one dropped
in the manner of falling while being held,
and touched in a manner hardly studious.
It drew over; it drew as a brunette
might draw her lunette up or down. There was
a moon. It was the substance of the dark.
They were beneath a cedar arbor, they were blonde,
and it was early summer. The arbor was a veil
of fragrance nailed up and down,
and it was through its braided surfaces the spider had appeared.
Impossible to say whether its threads were thrown between
or cast before, but some threads affixed a fine black dish
of apricots to limbs above their heads
or to heaven. Afterward, one feared
she hadn't set her face in a pleasing countenance
although she'd worn the yellow shawl,
and one actually left the sweetest flesh adhering to the pit
formerly said to be a stone, but first one spoke about the spider
and one wanted apricots, and each came speechless to their calm.

IMAGINARY LINES

When we said logic was transcendental,
we felt other words we might have said
find form the way shadows find form, with dependence
on things both intimately close and infinitely separate,
palpable as the sky palpating with a blue we saw
and loved and never felt surrounded by,
palpable as what we saw with our eyes closed.
We could feel the unsaid begin to touch our mouths
the same way shadows began first where two things met
and might be parted, where touch obscured
a body's edge so brilliantly.
How casually the light declined. The roundest pearls
gave way to oval shadows. Mornings we found
it snowed all night. There was often a feeling of rest gathering
to meet itself outside ourselves; there was the feeling
that thinking one thing had caused another thing to be.

CHEMIN DE FER

Why so much looked truer wet
we were never sure. Days after
our travels we would have to cry
to who loved us do you remember
from the moving train how the wet factory windows
warped into rows as a garment, as ribbons,
as a sleeve remembered with ribbon woven in, do you
remember those windows painted
green on the warehouse next,
where any sequence held the logic of magic:
this must have had to happen in this order
while we watched. That's how it was;
wasn't the sumac red on time, didn't that dog get across,
wasn't someone waiting whether we arrived or not.

FLIGHT OF STAIRS

Some pressed in just so, then stopped.
This was how we almost knew
the red flight of stairs
upward at the border crossing,
and the one pain realized
above the right shoulder blade,
momentary as the hair
of her begging there
with her dream touch,
how each dream accompanied
mere sleep, how we woke
at home, able to love red.

DAY OR NIGHT

We saw that the body of fire is triangular. We held
two hands before the breast; the left hand grasped a corner
of the stole, and the right hand, where thumb and index
touched, pressed upon the little finger of the left.
Of Fra Filippo's women on the stairs, we thought less
than of the one who must occur
to bear the god and lily-stalk. We believed
a flight of thought takes shape as real motion, even
in dream, where some dream-walked above dream-blooms
while others aged in a wakeful night of pain; that these,
occurring in a single night, made a place
where thoughts could catch, and move as something higher,
physical, where we could have an anodyne to close around
our furthest flowerings of pain, for we saw the heightened body
of the fire and quieted our hands at the level of our hearts,
and we saw, against sky blue or black, both the common and rare birds
flew easily above our thoughts, and were afraid of us.

WHITE SHELLS

Then there was beauty in what clung,
vertical and multiple against a damp tombstone
where no one goes, or has gone forever,
the stone carved in another language
and the weed-life overgrown.
We knew they must know movement,
but they would not move
while being what they meant to us.
Where the headstone's windowpane,
meant to protect the crucifix and photograph,
was cracked apart, we saw how
on its inward, wetter side,
the infant shells began self-generation in a line
like vowels strung inside a child's understanding:
this belongs to this. O perfect succulence
with which interiors adhere to forms, O open mouths.
Should we have found the world more often
clinging to words describing it?
What would have been the afterlife of that?

REGRET

We saw a woman, giant among us,
bend to retrieve a toy the dwarf-child dropped,
and we began to pose ourselves
among proportions, safe in our understanding
that the need to feel dominates the need to see,
and sure that each station of our lives
took its structure from a dream.
As if in dream, we saw a giant woman
bend to retrieve a toy the dwarf-child dropped.
We saw it roll as a pearl will, in one direction,
perfectly away. We didn't know
what we were guilty of. How flammable
the smallest sorrows are. From what great height
her drowsy arm poured down.

MANI

We wanted to think the stars were fed by fires
we'd made, so the memory of who we'd been
would be true as any object,
distinct, indelible, and half the time obscured.
Strange, it was from the depths of wetness
this seemed most possible, taken as we were
under the skin of water, looking at surface
from its underside, naming it heaven, or seeing
the fragile sparkling inside our lovers' mouths,
or calling on a prior thought: hadn't Euripides
named night the nursing mother of the stars?
How easily the world is filled with mouths
when one wants to eat. How few there are
at singing time. So, when the pearls
revealed themselves, or were revealed,
we were ashamed at having pried the shells
and said they had been found as thoughts
inside the brains of fish, or in the hearts of birds
always above our world. There were gestures:
the left hand forms a fist before the heart
and the right hand hovers over it, fingers
horizontal as a shore. We took the pearls
to be reversals of the progress
of our deaths, understood that they would fall
with our bodies when the veil dropped,
and we understood this meant return to fire.

BREATHLESS

Three finger-length bud vases, ruby glass, real
on the half lit windowsill, but in whose house?
Whose was their red air that didn't move,
in us like a voice saying *Lord, where are we
one with you?* And the Lord saying *where you are
no one's.*

THEOLOGY OF WATER

Water is a dampened flame. —Novalis
Water is a burned body. —Balzac

We said that water became holy, blessed by words.
There were closed vials of it, marvelous to hold
and through them the inverted world
was willed. This was the water of duration,
kept more often by the women than the men,
and among them, most often by the mothers.
We seemed as it seemed, more alive
the more time had to do with us,
though we were not preserved. How strange
to be led to thoughts of transformation
by something we ourselves arranged. If we loved to think
the saved water turned to tears, or became sweeter,
jewel-flavored, or more pure, it was to rehearse
our own transparency while moving palpably
across the earth like any night, though night was
uncontainable, was another habit of another thirst
we described as sleep. In our vials was
no sleep. Our holy water never slept;
it waited with our women to need us.

ST. FRANCIS ORPHANAGE, FREEPORT, ILLINOIS

The long view, understood as eaten
by the spring growth of fourteen junipers,
brought round an air of circumspection,
as when aggressive symmetry was broken by
a solemn picnic of clothed and nude figures
by Cézanne. Likewise, the foreground of the lawn
suggested itself as adequate, and was likewise wrong,
though who wouldn't be improved by having watched
the daily weakening of a small sea of thistle heads
once purple-pink on green, given to less,
given way. Less color, fewer butterflies:
pretty to notice and to say. A solemn picnic
of clothed men and naked women, stilled
but not thought of as still, and neither
did we look at them long.

SNOW HILL

It was as if the objects we described
were made heavier by words.
Then it seemed any person talking
could help an object bear its weight,
and that our lives could someday fill
with things made grand in increments
we'd later recognize as the source of a familiar voice,
as when snow falling on a hill amassed
for our desire the largest shapeliness,
while the sky revealed infinity with falling forms.
But when a mere displacement of the air
seemed to intensify the things
our mouths approached, as when a veil is
worried by a breath, or when we had been told
to part our mouths, we had no word, no song.
We feared what breathing was. Then
there was nothing to keep us from our final innocence,
nothing we would not have opened for.

CONTINUANCE

Then there was a place of no language
and we were afraid. We began to see
how arms were either raised or low,
hands held up or pendent,
and we began to know ourselves as shapes,
the edges of the flame to which we owed
existence, and we knew all things return to fire.
So the gestures of forms came into preciousness
as the singing of songs had once been dear,
or the sighing of our names.
So often the right hand was raised, palm out,
and the left kept low. It was the left hand
that we loved, which came to mean both fearlessness
and charity, though sometimes the fingers were upstretched
in the manner of outright offering, or
downstretched in the manner of conferring from above.
Then in late summer a moth from our childhood arrived,
an ochre Polyphemus, the "one-eyed giant,"
with each hind wing bearing a large eyespot
and each fore wing a smaller, as giant
as a sparrow among wrens. We began
forgetting the eyes of our dead
and knew nowhere to look to find what they had become.
Then what we knew of them was without name or form,
or even memory of form. Which was how the water opened
finally for us, and closed behind, and we entered the next change.

DULCE DE LECHE

We felt approached by afterthought
while listening, as an aspect of its pulse, but
something *summoned* that bright, brief
awareness of arrangements
as a close kind of beauty when
ascribed to the economy
of grammar. People are dead; what
is it to love sentences but the arrival
of the absolute bedrock of love?
In fall, to say the dove appears grass-colored
is not to say the grass brings on the colors of a dove.
In the horror of nonfeeling,
even toward those we were never going to meet,
could we begin to mend, admiring how a list
parades relationship, how it goes on?
I believe we were watching the closed eyes of someone
eating *dulce de leche* for the first time
when Larry of Nigeria, in his second
correspondence, wrote, *If things worked out fine
between us, I think I must considered
myself luck to have you,* which is so much what
we would like to have felt all the time. That, and
the obvious return of what we would have known.

JOY

We regretted the way to joy had been a labyrinth
of our making, where from interiors we'd made our way
further inside toward endings we could recognize
and turn back from. We'd invented the pocket labyrinth,
we trained our dogs to bark when we said speak,
we offered one another jewelry. But when the geckos
came inside for moths who'd found our lamps,
the joy we felt was magical, a violence of gentleness
apart from us that might revisit any night. Rare animals
are pink; small moths like these had changed to dust
while dying in the past. So it was terror kept awake in joy
that we began to feel rummaged by: there were
photographs of grandparents as youths,
there were fetishes: a fox, white in the face
where the stone was white, a bird made from a shell,
and a mole was carved from clearest quartz to magnify
the uselessness of sight. We could be struck dumb
by a small box made entirely of cloves and thread,
or by the relicarios where saints had been preserved
in two-inch portraits that were assemblages of feathers;
there were evenings the sky was lavender
and we were lost, there were dreams that recurred,
there was the same love you have now, and we were lost.

FROM THE SHORE

When we wondered what deserved the right
to be original, water rolled toward us
like a friend or sleep we had so long
practiced being entered by
we doubted it could help, but
this water was more motion
than substance after time,
was perfected as lifted
where it seemed to lift itself
like love making our bodies different.
We said thinking was moonlight. Feeling was
a wave, a field of waves, fresh in the instances
but with a sameness overall. In that wet air,
this seemed the depth of what our mood
allowed. At our upper limit was the moon.
At the bottom, under undulance, muscled in,
we trusted that the infant pearls were added to.

RED BIRD

We stopped believing we
could name the color of ascension,
and we learned to split the redness
from the cardinal's voice. But they
came near, especially in winter,
as an absolute comprised of many forms
we could, if not approach, be glad
for the existence of. It was when the inflection
of their song so often rose that we knew again
the correspondence of their visible and oral forms;
how could those who only sang by rising
not rise up? We were glad it was rare for us
to see them fall, but we trusted that they fell
quietly, while in their periphery, inflections
of our sentences continued their descents
from the time we were children who could speak,
who could be brought to weep even by the thought
of our own deaths. What secret had their bodies closed around,
brilliant there, singing up the disappearing song?

DATURA

The flower pod, green-white, hand-sized,
bloomed at night. As the dead increased,
the world of objects seemed more dense,
different from when our child-days dragged
or a sunflower's face, which, once arrived,
was heaviness itself. And it was different from
parenting, when days were thick,
years thin, or a poppy with a stem. There were
more cadences ascending and descending nearer by.
We saw one of us not reach
the hand-sized pod before it broke
into the mouth of an ordinary night,
though the hand reached toward,
as if a touch would enter it, end it,
or as though by touching what was strange
there was relief in being plain, or one might love
to cause an opening as when a blade cuts under blades of grass,
or words are said, or if a mouth opens another mouth. We saw
the hand fly back, the trumpet-petals curl. It was perverse
to be afraid; when the scent began, one leaned in again.

ABODE OF THE UNPLANNED EFFECT

What we kept, intensified. If we saw a mollusk, whole,
closed, and fossilized, we began to think of its pearl as a better pearl
for having been removed from the burden of a public life;
when we invited guests into our homes, we loved to step
outside and look in at the bodies crossing rooms
where our objects lay in drawers our guests would never open,
and if the flowering shrub beside us was contained
by the same scent as in a former year, we were contained by
thinking so. When our sadness died with greater beauty
than our joy, sorrow seemed a room we could approach
and we were glad to be alone,
enclosed with all the exhalations of our former visitors
to feel the sun occluded, then radiant, then gone,
and the night in all its variation, until to be enclosed
was an embrace we knew as otherworldly, composed
of flickerings from far outside ourselves, an embrace
that tightened at the peak of every inhalation
until we were wild for love.

MOTHER-OF-PEARL

Afterward it seemed time to think of memory,
as though two coat pockets emptied of the empty halves
of thumbnail-sized bivalves could be the final outer fragments
of a delicate, essential, boneless understanding,
succulent, but to whom, like brains or tongue, an understanding
intelligent with creature comfort like a former nest for wasps
or a hand-sized basket with black spiders woven in,
keeping still the thought of her who hung
headlong in mostly air above a door last fall,
or like the flush we felt, accepting graciously a fingerling
carving of a snake, when a snake itself, even such a short one,
would bring on the customary fear; it seemed time to see something
as something prior to itself, pearly without pearls, mother-of-pearl.

TREE AND SAW

When its stillness was felt to be a kind of waiting,
the saw seemed able. Accordingly, the tree
seemed finally capable of sight, as though
watching was another of its properties
kept hidden with its root or viscous center.
The saw was felt to still itself by having gathered
past and future rivenings toward the assembly of
a hope. The tree was thought to see exactly what was
other than itself: daylight flung across a wall
pierced by a window, whereby perspective issued
back and forth. We said we felt like saws
made heavier with waiting. We were trees
buoyant with sight, fit to be passed through.
We knew our cupboards painted red occurred
as embers in the late striking of those days.

PEARL, NO PEARL

One cannot fly into flying. —Nietzche

We found no final thought worked onto matter,
no end for slow lives churned into appearance so
solemn, terrestrial, thalassic, lapidary, they seemed
to have moved into stillness by being still...
O and the coldest, inmost honey,
yellow, white, good, ice-fresh, golden,
thinned, being lit by us,
alighted on by our eyes
without scent, like pearls,
without memory of scent, like pearls;
O we might have been
sweet with the iridescence of an infinite idea
but we could be no pearl, no
pearl. No honey and no pearl.

APART

Nine pearls rolled in the hand
sound like no other thing. One less
and the change was indiscernible,
except the one removed was what
we thought about. We could sense
the coming exhalation when one breath
crossed into another body in a kiss, even
in a dream. What left us, we magnified
to keep ourselves aware things could, and had been
changed, though we appeared ungrateful for
our eight pearls. We expected who could see us
would perceive. Which is how we could bear
the junipers shagged with ice,
and the lark. Some singing cracked the air apart;
we hoped the single pearl belonged to sea again.

VERTIGO

Where we said the blooms were heads,
the field of thistles broke open into pink again,
and again the heads were further beautified
by the just born white-winged summer butterflies,
but why each butterfly faced west while eating there, again,
we couldn't say; we felt excluded as a friend whose friend
stands privately apart as plates are gently filled and gently emptied,
gently washed; we were aware that when we thought of vertigo
as the constant realm between all separated bodies, we felt vertiginous,
and when we thought it lay exterior to any bodies intertwined,
we felt the same unease. We found no world apart from falling, no world
we could fall from. Touching the thistle field, we heard our dying and
our lovesick try again to sing *let the living feed the living, let the dead.*
There will be pearls that will have been our eyes
and brides enough to carry them.

RETURN

The hand is lowered, the palm turned up
in a gesture of offering, the palm
completely exposed, open
and empty, the fingers lightly bent
as if they had supported something round, as if a soft stone
had just been passed on to a hand of someone loved,
the stone halved and hollowed,
then closed around a laurel pod
still containing its one seed. To hear a seed
move in its pod inside a hollow stone brings on
a holy flex of possibilities we understood as
more than double joy; it made a good arrangement
between us and our deaths; it formed a layered world,
better than a blended one, the bidden moving
inside the forbidden, or the bidden kept still,
but it was given, and made,
and it was right the way the empty hand reminded us.

QUICK TO FLY

And then the pearl was obsolete. And the feeling was
that we had arrived too late for an event
that might have healed us had we not
marked ourselves with fragile things,
or we had arrived too early for the same event
and, being so easily undone,
to finish was beyond our reach.
The obsolescence of all pearliness was absolute
while the occasions to feel were still particular, were felt
to be real in a concave way, as when a middle name
was overheard as the first name of someone else,
or a kiss occurred in dream, or we felt nicked by the shadow
of a passerby, or in the way we felt passed into by some scents:
creosote on the walkway to Singingbird Lodge,
winter river, lit match, pine sap. Truly,
we felt the absence also in convex ways,
as when the dreamer was a child, or a bird flew
from inside a house, or an egg was found outside,
whole and rolled away. We sensed the lark
in each larkspur. We felt we should be grateful, and we were.

NOTES & ACKNOWLEDGEMENTS

Thanks to the editors of the following journals, in which some of these poems first appeared:

American Literary Review: "St. Francis Orphanage, Freeport, Illinois," "Pearl, No Pearl," "Accession," "Vertigo,"
Blackbird: "From Inside," "From the Middle," "From Underneath," "Measure."
Field: "Slow Song."
The Laurel Review: "The Bells Break Down Their Tower."
The Paris Review: "Dreaming of Sleep," "Jaws," "Imaginary Lines," "Datura."
Pequod: "Linen Napkin."
River City: "Apart."
The Western Humanities Review: "Dulce de Leche."
Xantippe: "Tree and Saw," "Snow Hill," "Flight of Stairs."

"Fondle Pearls and They're Quick to Fly" takes its title from the second line of Meng Chiao's poem series, "Apricots Died Young," translated by David Hinton.

The title "Time Shall Not Lose Our Passages" is a line from Donne's 12th elegy.

"The Bells Break Down Their Tower" takes its title from a line of Hart Crane's poem, "The Broken Tower."

The first line of "Jaws" is from Rilke's "Tombs of the Heterae," translated by Stephen Mitchell.

Delectatio morosa: a temptation to which medieval monks were susceptible, an obsession that comes from a profound and sustained concentration on recurring forms and ideas—the idea becomes part of the thinker's body; he returns to it over and over again. Also, in Catholicism, one of the three kinds of internal sin: the pleasure taken in a sinful thought or imagination even without desiring it.

"Mani" is Sanskrit for pearl.

"Theology of Water" shares its title with Johann Albert Fabricius' 1741 text, *Theologie de L'eau.*

The St. Francis Orphanage in Freeport, Illinois, is where my grandfather, Frank Kemp, spent most of his childhood.

"Continuance:" *"Each thing is merely the limit of the flame to which it owes its existence."* —Rodin

"Abode of the Unplanned Effect" is also the title of a poem by T'ao Ch'ien, translated by David Hinton.

"Tree and Saw" is for Carl Rice Embrey.

Line six of "Pearl, No Pearl," is from Neitzche's "The Honey Sacrifice" in *Thus Spoke Zarathustra,* translated by Walter Kauffmann.

"Black Pearl," "Continuance," "Day or Night," and "Return" contain descriptions of hand gestures found in *Mudra: A Study of Symbolic Gestures in Japanese Buddhist Sculpture,* by E. Dale Saunders.

Phrasing is sometimes culled from essays by Gaston Bachelard, especially *The Psychoanalysis of Fire,* translated by C. M. Ross, *Air and Dreams: An Essay On the Imagination of Movement,* and *Water and Dreams: An Essay On the Imagination of Matter,* both translated by Edith R. Farrell and C. Frederick Farrell.